Let Freedom Ring

Francis Scott Key

Patriotic Poet

by Susan R. Gregson

Consultant:
Scott Sheads
Historian/Librarian
Fort McHenry National Monument
National Park Service
Baltimore, Maryland

Bridgestone Books
an imprint of Capstone Press
Mankato, Minnesota

Bridgestone Books are published by Capstone Press
151 Good Counsel Drive, P.O. Box 669, Mankato, Minnesota 56002
http://www.capstone-press.com

Printed in the United States of America

Library of Congress Cataloging-in-Publication Data
Gregson, Susan R.
    Francis Scott Key: patriotic poet / by Susan R. Gregson.
    p. cm. — (Let freedom ring)
    Summary: Describes the life of the lawyer and poet, Francis Scott Key, best known for writing the poem "The Star-Spangled Banner" in 1814.
    Includes bibliographical references and index.
    ISBN 0-7368-1554-6
    1. Key, Francis Scott, 1779–1843—Juvenile literature. 2. Poets, American—19th century—Biography—Juvenile literature. 3. United States—History—War of 1812—Biography—Juvenile literature. 4. Patriotic poetry, American—Authorship—Juvenile literature. 5. Star-spangled banner (Song)—Juvenile literature. [1. Key, Francis Scott, 1779–1843. 2. Poets. 3. Lawyers. 4. Star-spangled banner (Song)] I. Title. II. Series.
PS2168.G74 2003
811'.2—dc21
                                                            2002011703

Editorial Credits
Kremena Spengler, editor; Kia Adams, series designer; Juliette Peters, book designer; Angi Gahler, Illustrator; Kelly Garvin, photo researcher; Karen Risch, product planning editor

Photo Credits
Corbis, 31, Corbis/Bettmann, 6, 10, 23, Corbis/Lee Snider, 13, Corbis/Yogi, Inc., 35
David Gardner, 38
Getty Images/M. David Leeds, 41
Library of Congress, cover (inset), 5, 32
Naval Undersea Museum, 40
North Wind Picture Archives, 9, 11, 15, 16, 18-19, 24, 27, 28, 43
PhotoSpin, 37, 40
Stock Montage, Inc., cover

1   2   3   4   5   6   08   07   06   05   04   03

Table of Contents

Chapter One

The Man Who Wrote the Anthem

On September 13 and 14, 1814, Francis Scott Key watched the British navy bomb Fort McHenry. The fort defended Baltimore, Maryland, and the British wanted to capture the city. The 35-year-old Francis was in a small American boat towed by a large British warship. British sailors earlier had taken the small boat's sails. They wanted to keep a U.S. government official, a doctor, and Francis from escaping to tell the Americans about the British plan to attack Fort McHenry.

When the bombing stopped and the smoke cleared, Francis looked through a small telescope. The U.S. flag was still flying over Fort McHenry. Francis was relieved that the Americans had held off the British.

In 1814, Francis watched the British bomb Fort McHenry. The event inspired him to write the poem called "The Star-Spangled Banner."

In 1814, this flag flew over Fort McHenry, inspiring Francis to write the national anthem.

Flag Restoration

The flag that inspired Francis to write the national anthem is in the Smithsonian National Museum of American History in Washington, D.C. In 1996, the museum started a special project to restore and preserve the fading flag. More than 4 million people have watched workers repair the flag in a special lab. When the restoration is complete, the flag will appear in a new exhibit called "For Which It Stands."

Francis scribbled the first part of a poem on a piece of paper. The poem became a song called "The Star-Spangled Banner." More than a century later, Congress and the president made the song the U.S. national anthem.

People remember Francis Scott Key as the man who wrote the anthem. He was also a father, lawyer, religious leader, and public servant.

Chapter Two

Young Francis

Francis Scott Key was born on August 1, 1779, in Frederick County, Maryland. He lived on a large farm called Terra Rubra. Francis grew up with his sister Anne. Their parents were John Ross Key and Anne Phoebe Penn Dagworthy Charlton Key.

The Keys were a wealthy family with servants and slaves. Francis' father fought in the Revolutionary War (1775–1783). He paid for uniforms and weapons for the soldiers in his battle unit. Like his father, Francis would one day fight in a war.

School Days

When Francis was 10 years old, he traveled to the city of Annapolis, Maryland, to attend school. He lived with his blind grandmother, Ann Arnold Ross Key. She had been blinded when she was

Francis was born to wealthy parents in Frederick County, Maryland. This portrait shows Francis as a young man.

young, rescuing two servants from her father's burning house.

Beginning in 1789, Francis attended the College of St. John's in Annapolis. In Francis' time, St. John's had both a grammar school for younger children and college courses for older students.

Records show that Francis got into a great deal of mischief. Once he let a cow loose across the school's lawn. He also played tricks on teachers the students did not like. He was known for making up silly songs about people.

Francis grew up in this house on a large Maryland farm called Terra Rubra.

Roger Brooke Taney

Roger Brooke Taney was one of
Francis' best friends. They met
when both men were young
lawyers. Taney later became
Chief Justice of the U.S.
Supreme Court. Justice Taney
issued the famous Dred Scott
decision. Taney wrote that slaves
did not deserve any rights.

Still, Francis found time to study. When he
graduated from St. John's at age 17, he was first in
his class of 12 people.

The Call of Law

In 1800, the slender, blue-eyed Francis began to
study law. Both his father and uncle Philip Barton
were lawyers. Uncle Philip helped Francis get a
position to study law under a judge. Francis met

Francis' Family

Francis and his wife Mary Tayloe Lloyd Key had 11 children. They had six boys and five girls. Three sons died young. One accidentally drowned when he was 6 years old. One son was killed in a duel, and another one died at age 28 of an unknown illness.

one of his best friends, Roger Brooke Taney, while he worked with the judge. Taney later married Francis' sister, Anne.

In 1801, Francis opened his own law practice with Taney in Frederick, Maryland. In 1802, Francis married Mary Tayloe Lloyd, the daughter of a well-known colonel in Annapolis. Francis called his wife Polly. He wrote funny poems to her and family members. Francis and Polly had 11 children. In 1804, the Keys moved to Georgetown, near Washington, D.C. Georgetown was still part of Maryland then.

In Georgetown, Francis went into law practice with his uncle Philip. Their law practice grew.

Georgetown was a busy city of 4,000 to 5,000 people. It was located just a few miles from the U.S. Capitol building and the president's Executive Mansion, now called the White House.

Francis practiced law with Roger Brooke Taney at this office in Frederick, Maryland.

Chapter Three

Signs of War

By the early 1800s, the U.S. relationship with Great Britain had been worsening for several years. The British were supposed to remove their forts after the Revolutionary War. Instead, they left forts around the Great Lakes and Canada.

Great Britain was at war with France and needed seamen. The British dragged American men from their ships and put them to work on British ships. This practice was called impressment. The British mistreated the Americans, and tensions rose between the two countries. Then, both France and Great Britain began to block American trade with other countries.

In the early 1800s, the British took American men from their ships and put them to work on British ships.

War Is Declared

On the western frontier of the United States, the British were giving guns and food to American Indians. Shawnee Chief Tecumseh and his followers joined the British. The British hoped American Indians would attack settlers moving west through the wilderness. American settlers also feared the British might attack through Canada.

During the War of 1812, Shawnee Chief Tecumseh and his followers joined the British side. Chief Tecumseh is shown here wearing a British army uniform.

"Old Ironsides"

The British navy had more than 1,000 ships at the start of the War of 1812. The United States had fewer than 20. The USS *Constitution* won the first naval battle in the war. Sailors called the ship "Old Ironsides" because cannonballs bounced off its side. The *Constitution* never lost a battle during 84 years as a warship. The ship is now a museum in Boston's harbor.

In 1810, many men from southern farm states and the west were elected to Congress. They spoke for settlers who were struggling because they were unable to sell their crops overseas or feared British and Indian attacks. More Americans began to call for a war with Great Britain. On June 18, 1812, Congress declared war on Great Britain. It was called the War of 1812 (1812–1814).

Francis Objects to War

At first, Francis was against the war. He was active in the Episcopal Church. The church's influence led him to believe that war was wrong. Francis did not believe the United States was going to war to settle the problems with impressment and selling U.S. goods overseas. He believed that politicians wanted to take Canada from the British.

Francis changed his mind when British soldiers and sailors landed in the United States. He was ready to fight. In 1813, he joined other citizens training to fight and served in the

During the War of 1812, many men, including Francis, served as volunteer soldiers in the militia.

Georgetown militia for about 10 days. Francis helped load, fire, and clean the cannons. He was not very good at the job.

A Lawyer Becomes a Soldier

In the summer of 1814, the courts closed because of the war. Lawyers were not needed. Francis joined the militia again. He gathered food and horses from nearby farmers to help the militia. Stories say he was not forceful enough to get the supplies from the farmers. He was also clumsy. In a letter to a friend, Francis said he tumbled over his horse's head once

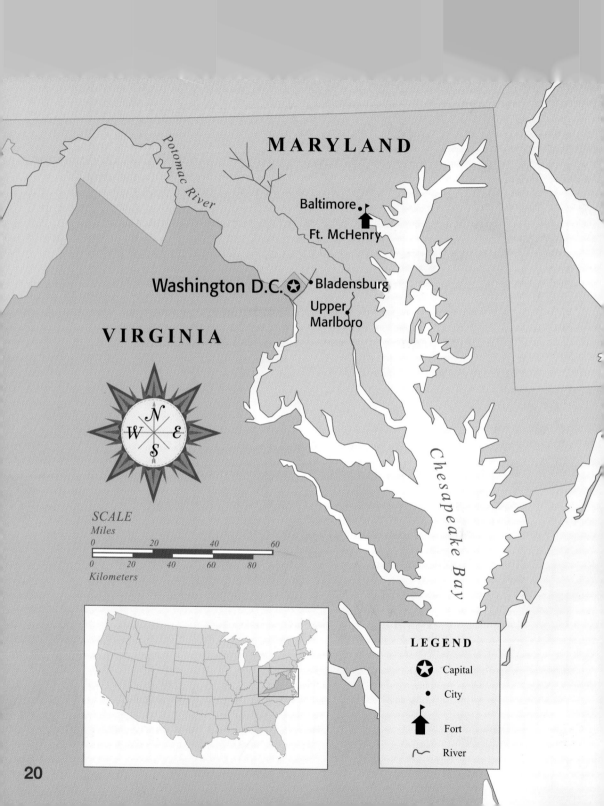

MARYLAND

Potomac River

Baltimore
Ft. McHenry

Washington D.C.
Bladensburg

Upper
Marlboro

VIRGINIA

N
W E
S

Chesapeake Bay

SCALE
Miles
0   20   40   60

0   20   40   60   80
Kilometers

LEGEND

⭐ Capital

• City

⬆ Fort

~ River

and landed in a river. Another time, someone accidentally hit him in the face with a piece of pork.

When the British were preparing to attack Washington, D.C., Francis served as an aide to a general. In 1813, Americans had burned York, Canada, which is now Toronto. In response, British soldiers landed near Washington, D.C., on August 24, 1814. The British defeated the American soldiers and militia during the Battle of Bladensburg, Maryland, which is also called the Battle of Washington. Most of the Americans ran away from the British. Francis was unhurt.

The British Burn Washington

British soldiers marched from Bladensburg into Washington, D.C., and burned government buildings. The people who lived in Washington, D.C., left without defending the city. President James Madison and his wife, Dolley, left the Executive Mansion so quickly that they abandoned dinner on the table. The British officers ate the dinner before they set fire to the building. They then turned their attention to Baltimore, Maryland.

Chapter Four

Bombs Bursting in Air

After the Battle of Bladensburg, Francis returned to his home in Georgetown. Within a week, he learned that British soldiers had arrested his old friend Dr. William Beanes. British troops who fought in the Battle of Bladensburg had received care in nearby Upper Marlboro, where Dr. Beanes lived. After the troops left, three soldiers stayed in the town.

These soldiers went to a party at Dr. Beanes' home. They were rowdy and demanded wine. Dr. Beanes had them arrested and thrown in jail. The British rescued the soldiers and took Dr. Beanes along as a prisoner. They kept him on a British ship, the HMS *Tonnant*.

Francis rode to the house in Washington, D.C., where President Madison was staying since the burning of the Executive Mansion.

In 1814, Francis sailed to the British ships to try to free his friend Dr. William Beanes. Francis watched the British navy bomb Fort McHenry.

Francis asked for the president's permission to go to the British and ask them to free Dr. Beanes. President Madison agreed and told Francis to take Colonel John Skinner. Skinner was the government officer who worked to get prisoners freed.

Francis Sails for the Warships

Colonel Skinner was in Baltimore. The city was busy preparing to defend itself against the British. A thousand men were sinking ships in the water around Fort McHenry to keep the British warships

British warships blockaded the Chesapeake Bay and prepared to attack Fort McHenry from the sea.

The Bombing of Fort McHenry

The British bombed Fort McHenry for 25 hours. Sailors on British warships fired more than 1,500 shells and rockets at the fort. Only four Americans died in the battle.

away. Small gunboats were set up in the water. People dug long, narrow ditches called trenches and put sandbags all around the city. Militia hid in the woods to attack the British foot soldiers.

Francis and Colonel Skinner had to wait for a storm to pass. On September 5, 1814, they set sail in a small boat. They flew a white flag to show they were peaceful and headed for the Chesapeake Bay. Aboard the *Tonnant*, British officers listened to Francis argue for Dr. Beanes' release. Vice Admiral Sir Alexander Cochrane and Rear Admiral George Cockburn said no to Francis.

Francis had brought letters from British soldiers. The letters said that American doctors had treated the wounded soldiers kindly after the Battle of Bladensburg. Major General Robert Ross was moved by the letters.

Myth versus Fact

The flag that flew over Fort McHenry during the British bombing was not the flag that Francis saw at dawn on September 14, 1814. It was raining during the battle, and the fort commander flew a smaller storm flag. At dawn, he flew the larger flag so people could see it from far away.

The Battle Begins

General Ross was co-commander of the British forces, and he freed Dr. Beanes. Later, a rifleman killed General Ross as he marched his troops toward Baltimore. The British kept Francis, Colonel Skinner, and Dr. Beanes until after the attack on Fort McHenry. The British navy did not want the men to reveal the plan of attack, so they took the American boat's sails. The bombing began at sunrise on September 13, 1814.

Bombs whistled through the air. Exploding rockets lit the sky. Francis was worried. He stood on his boat and looked for the U.S. flag flying over Fort

McHenry. Night fell, and the men could see the flag only when a rocket lit the sky.

Dawn's Early Light

At dawn the next day, Francis looked through his pocket telescope and saw the U.S. flag flying from the fort. He began to write a poem on a piece of paper in his pocket. The Americans had won. Francis, Colonel Skinner, and Dr. Beanes were allowed to leave. When the men got to Baltimore, Francis finished the poem in his hotel room.

Rear Admiral George Cockburn led the British troops who burned government buildings in Washington, D.C.

The Star-Spangled Banner.

O say! can you see by the dawn's early light
What so proudly we hail'd at the twilight's last gleaming
Whose broad stripes and bright stars, through the clouds of the fight,
O'er the ramparts we watch'd were so gallantly streaming?
And the rocket's red glare - the bomb bursting in air
Gave proof through the night that our flag was still there?
O say, does that star-spangled banner yet wave
O'er the land of the free & the home of the brave? –

FAC-SIMILE OF THE ORIGINAL MANUSCRIPT OF THE FIRST STANZA OF "THE STAR-SPANGLED BANNER."

"The Star-Spangled Banner," which Francis wrote on a piece of paper, was immediately popular. The original words were slightly different from the words sung today.

Looking for a Printer

Judge Joseph Hopper Nicholson, a relative of Francis' and the second-in-command at Fort McHenry, traveled all over Baltimore the day after the battle to find someone to print Francis' poem. The city was still getting back on its feet after the battle. Most of the print shops were closed. A 14-year-old helper at one shop, Samuel Sands, said he could print a small booklet. Young Samuel printed the title "The Defence of Fort M'Henry." People later called the song "The Star-Spangled Banner."

The poem was first printed on a single sheet of paper and called "The Defence of Fort M'Henry." It was to be sung to the tune of an old English drinking song that was popular in the United States, called "To Anacreon in Heaven." A few months later, people were calling Francis' song "The Star-Spangled Banner." The song was popular immediately.

Chapter Five

From War to Peace

The War of 1812 ended, and more settlers moved west. The U.S. government pushed the American Indian nations onto reservations. Trade was open again between the United States and other countries. Francis and his family stayed in Georgetown. Francis thought about becoming a preacher but returned to his law office instead.

After the war, Francis enjoyed times at home with his family. He was deeply religious and led his family and servants in prayer twice a day. The children played on the large lawn of the family property. One spring, Francis asked the gardener to plant a patch of flowers for each child. When the flowers appeared, the blooms outlined each child's name.

After the War of 1812 ended, Francis and his family resumed their peaceful lives in Georgetown.

Legal and Community Life

An excellent speaker, Francis often appeared before the U.S. Supreme Court to argue cases. In the mid-1830s, the Keys moved from Georgetown to

Francis and his family lived in this house in the early 1800s.

Dealing with Slavery

Francis and his wife owned slaves. He let some go free, but he did not think slavery was wrong. He worried that no one would take care of his slaves when they got older. Francis helped create the American Colonization Society. The group worked to send slaves to Africa to begin a free country there. Most slaves did not want to go to Africa because they were born in the United States. Many people did not like what the society was trying to do.

Washington, D.C. From 1833 to 1841, Francis served as the district attorney for the District of Columbia. President Andrew Jackson trusted Francis. Jackson sent Francis on special trips to work out agreements with people. Once, Francis traveled to Alabama. He worked to settle an argument between the state and federal governments about Creek Indian land.

When he did not work as a lawyer, Francis helped his community. He helped organize a society

The Missing House

Francis' house in Georgetown, Maryland, was lost. In 1947, the National Park Service took the house apart to build a new highway. The park service stored the woodwork and stonework. A year later, Congress set money aside to restore the house, but President Harry Truman said no. Most people forgot about the house. In 1985, the Francis Scott Key Foundation posted a reward for information on the "missing house." The park service said it had probably thrown away the woodwork. Someone had stolen the bricks. A writer in *People* magazine said, "Anyone can lose house keys, but it takes the government to lose Key's house."

to educate poor children. He organized several religious groups. Francis helped create a society that tried to deal with the country's slavery issue.

Francis Dies

On January 11, 1843, Francis died of pneumonia at the Baltimore home of one of his daughters. Before his death, he told his wife about money in a leather bag that he wanted given to charity. Francis was buried in St. Paul's Cemetery in Baltimore. In 1866, his body was moved to Mount Olivet Cemetery in Frederick, Maryland.

Francis was a good father, gifted speaker, and talented lawyer. He fought for his country during the War of 1812. He served in public office during peace time. Francis gave his time and money to his community. Still, most people remember him for the anthem that helped the nation honor its flag.

This statue of Francis Scott Key marks his gravesite in Mount Olivet Cemetery in Frederick, Maryland.

Chapter Six

Long May It Wave

"The Star-Spangled Banner" remained popular through changing times. People in the North and South played it during the Civil War (1861–1865). In 1889, the navy secretary ordered the song played at flag ceremonies. In the 1890s, the U.S. Army and Navy made "The Star-Spangled Banner" their official song. In 1916, President Woodrow Wilson began using the song at official events. More than 40 laws introduced in the 1900s asked Congress to make the song the national anthem.

"The Banner" or Not "The Banner"

Not everyone liked "The Star-Spangled Banner." The song's high and low notes are difficult to sing. Some people did not like the song because it was set to the music of a drinking song. They believed it set a bad example. Others thought the

"The Star-Spangled Banner" is the world's only national anthem written about a flag.

words would make children think that war was the only place to find heroes. Some people wanted "Yankee Doodle" or "America the Beautiful" to become the country's anthem.

The first monument to Francis opened in 1888 in Golden Gate Park in San Francisco, California. His grandchildren and more than 10,000 other people attended the ceremony.

In His Own Words

"I saw the flag of my country waving over a city... I witnessed the preparation for its assaults. I saw the array of its enemies as they advanced to the attack. I heard the sound of battle. The noise of the conflict fell upon my listening ear and told me that the brave and the free had met the invaders." — Francis Scott Key, in a speech given many years after he wrote the anthem

In the 1920s, war veterans came together and worked to get lawmakers to pick "The Star-Spangled Banner." Other groups joined in the movement. By 1930, the Veterans of Foreign Wars (VFW) organization had gathered the names of 5 million Americans who wanted "The Star-Spangled Banner" to be the national anthem. Finally, a law passed through Congress, and President Herbert Hoover signed it. On March 3, 1931, "The Star-Spangled Banner" became the U.S. national anthem.

The USS *Francis Scott Key*

The USS *Francis Scott Key* was a submarine built in 1964. In 1993, it was taken out of service. Its metal was later used for other projects.

Francis' Lasting Gift

"The Star-Spangled Banner" is the only national anthem in the world written about a flag. Many people feel a strong love for their country when they see the flag and hear the anthem. In times of trouble, the flag and the music bring Americans together. "The Star-Spangled Banner" and the way it can make people feel good about their country is Francis Scott Key's everlasting gift to the nation.

Today, the national anthem is played at the start of sporting events.
Only the first verse is sung.

TIMELINE

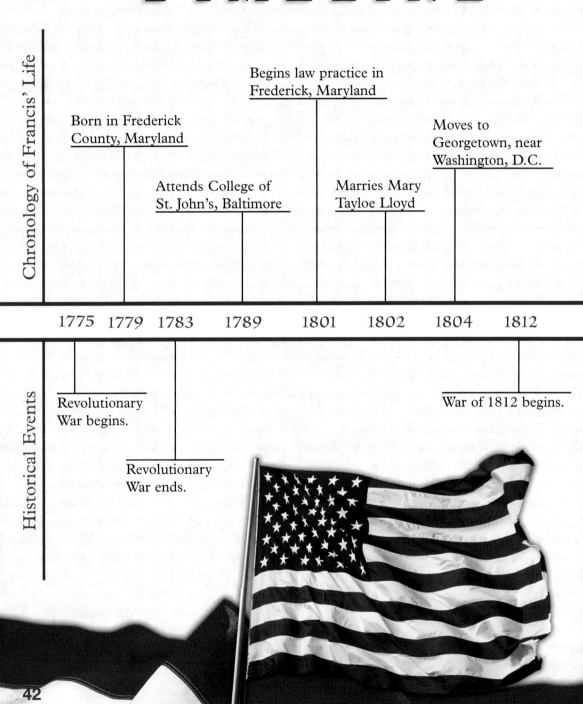

Chronology of Francis' Life

Begins law practice in
Frederick, Maryland

Born in Frederick
County, Maryland

Attends College of
St. John's, Baltimore

Marries Mary
Tayloe Lloyd

Moves to
Georgetown, near
Washington, D.C.

1775   1779   1783   1789   1801   1802   1804   1812

Historical Events

Revolutionary
War begins.

Revolutionary
War ends.

War of 1812 begins.

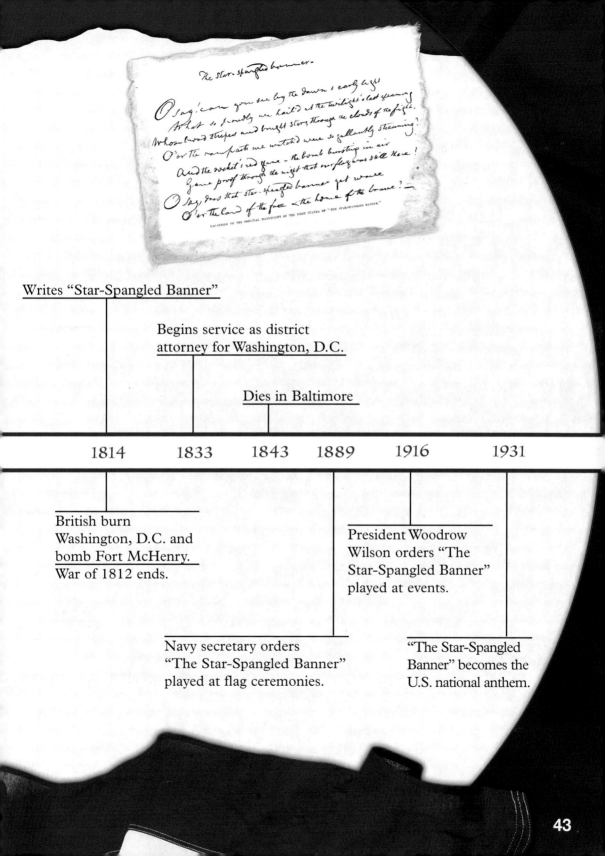

The Star-Spangled Banner.

O say! can you see by the dawn's early light
What so proudly we hail'd at the twilight's last gleaming,
Whose broad stripes and bright stars, through the clouds of the fight,
O'er the ramparts we watch'd were so gallantly streaming?
And the rocket's red glare—the bomb bursting in air,
Gave proof through the night that our flag was still there!
O say, does that star-spangled banner yet wave
O'er the land of the free & the home of the brave? —

FAC-SIMILE OF THE ORIGINAL MANUSCRIPT OF THE FIRST STANZA OF "THE STAR-SPANGLED BANNER."

Writes "Star-Spangled Banner"

Begins service as district
attorney for Washington, D.C.

Dies in Baltimore

| 1814 | 1833 | 1843 | 1889 | 1916 | 1931 |

British burn
Washington, D.C. and
bomb Fort McHenry.
War of 1812 ends.

President Woodrow
Wilson orders "The
Star-Spangled Banner"
played at events.

Navy secretary orders
"The Star-Spangled Banner"
played at flag ceremonies.

"The Star-Spangled
Banner" becomes the
U.S. national anthem.

Glossary

anthem (AN-thuhm)—a song of honor or praise

frontier (fruhn-TIHR)—the edge of a country where few people live

impressment (im-PRESS-muhnt)—forcing sailors into service

militia (muh-LISH-uh)—a group of volunteer citizens who are trained to fight battles

patriot (PAY-tree-uht)—a person loyal to and proud of his or her country

spangled (SPANG-guhld)—covered with bright objects, such as stars

trench (TRENCH)—a long, narrow ditch; Soldiers fight in trenches during wars.

twilight (TWY-lite)—dim light outside at sunrise or sunset

For Further Reading

Bennett, William J. ed. *The Children's Book of America.* New York: Simon & Schuster, 1998.

Haberle, Susan E. *The War of 1812.* Let Freedom Ring. Mankato, Minn.: Bridgestone Books, 2003.

Hakim, Joy. *The New Nation.* History of U.S. New York: Oxford University Press, 2003.

Quiri, Patricia Ryon. *The National Anthem.* A True Book. New York: Children's Press, 1998.

Weber, Michael. *The Young Republic.* Making of America. Austin, Texas: Raintree Steck Vaughn, 2000.

Places of Interest

Fort McHenry National Monument and Historic Shrine
East Fort Avenue
Baltimore, MD 21230-5393
Fort McHenry is the site of the War of 1812 battle against British warships that inspired Key to write the national anthem.

Maryland Historical Society
201 West Monument Street
Baltimore, MD 21201-4674
The society has the original "Star-Spangled Banner" manuscript and a collection of items from the War of 1812.

Mount Olivet Cemetery
Market Street
Frederick, MD 21701
This is the location of Francis' grave and monument.

National Museum of American History, Behring Center
Smithsonian Institution
14th Street and Constitution Avenue NW
Washington, DC 20001
Visitors can watch the restoration of the original flag that inspired Francis to write the anthem.

Terra Rubra Farm
Keysville-Bruceville Road
Carroll County
Keymar, MD 21757
Since 1949, the U.S. flag has flown continuously over a monument at Terra Rubra farm, the site of Francis' birthplace.

USS *Constitution* Museum
Boston, MA 02101
A hands-on museum near and aboard the USS *Constitution* allows visitors to explore the oldest active warship in the United States.

Internet Sites

Do you want to learn more about Francis Scott Key?
Visit the FACT HOUND at *http://www.facthound.com*

FACT HOUND can track down many sites to help you.
All the FACT HOUND sites are hand-selected
by Capstone Press editors. FACT HOUND will fetch the best,
most accurate information to answer your questions.

IT IS EASY! IT IS FUN!
1) Go to *http://www.facthound.com*
2) Type in: 0736815546
3) Click on "Fetch It" and FACT HOUND
   will put you on the trail
   of several helpful links.

You can also search by subject or book title. So, relax
and let our pal FACT HOUND do the research for you!

Index